HORRIBLE THINGS

Bizarre, Creepy Hoaxes

by Kelly Regan Barnhill

Consultant:
David D. Gilmore
Professor of Anthropology
Stony Brook University
Stony Brook, New York

Capstone press®

Mankato, Minnesota

Edge Books are published by Capstone Press,
151 Good Counsel Drive, P.O. Box 669, Mankato, Minnesota 56002.
www.capstonepress.com

Library of Congress Cataloging-in-Publication Data
Barnhill, Kelly Regan.
    Bizarre creepy hoaxes / by Kelly Regan Barnhill.
    p. cm. — (Edge books. Horrible things)
    Includes bibliographical references and index.
    Summary: "Describes a variety of famous hoaxes from
the past" — Provided by publisher.
    ISBN-13: 978-1-4296-2294-3 (hardcover)
    ISBN-10: 1-4296-2294-6 (hardcover)
    1. Impostors and imposture — Juvenile literature. 2. Fraud —
Juvenile literature. 3. Deception — Juvenile literature. I. Title.
HV6751.B37 2009
001.9'5 — dc22   2008028707

Editorial Credits
Aaron Sautter, editor; Ted Williams, designer; Jo Miller, photo researcher

Photo Credits
Alamy/Philip Scalia, 29
AP Images/John Bazemore, 14; Thomas Grimm, 20
Capstone Press, 15, 26; Karon Dubke, 4
Corbis/Richard Hamilton Smith, 24
Dan Baines 2007 - www.lebanoncircle.co.uk, 13
Fortean Picture Library, 10
Getty Images Inc./Martin Klimek, 27; Popperfoto, 8, 16;
    Taxi/David McGlynn, 6; Time Life Pictures/Amy Etra, 17
The Granger Collection, New York/Rue des Archives, 7;
    New York/ullstein bild, 23
The Image Works/SSPL, cover
Mary Evans Picture Library, 18
Newscom, 19

1 2 3 4 5 6 14 13 12 11 10 09

Table of Contents

Look Behind the Curtain

"Step right up ladies and gentlemen, and see the wonders of the world! You'll gasp! You'll weep! You'll tremble with amazement! For just one dollar, you can see the incredible sights right behind the curtain!"

Clever hoaxers often use words like this to get people to pay money to see shocking things. But their job is to fool you. They invent tall tales about weird animals and odd people. They trick people into spending their hard-earned money to see fake creatures and **artifacts**.

Yet hoaxers' tales often sound believable. The cleverest hoaxers often blend a little truth with their lies. This way, they're able to fool lots of people. Let's take a look behind the curtain and explore history's most outrageous hoaxes.

artifact — an object made and used by people in the past

1

Psychics

Fortune-tellers often claim to see the future in crystal balls.

Feel like paying money for lies? Lots of people do it. They pay **psychics** to read their palms, look into a crystal ball, or read tarot cards. Can these people really look into the future? Most scientists don't think so. They say there is no way to predict future events.

psychic — someone who claims to be able to tell the future

The most famous fortune-teller in history was Nostradamus. In the mid-1500s, Nostradamus wrote hundreds of predictions. But his writings are very vague. Nobody has ever been able to plan for future events based on his predictions. However, sometimes events seem very similar to what Nostradamus predicted hundreds of years ago. When this happens, some people believe he really saw the future.

GUIDED BY THE STARS

Even world leaders sometimes get advice from fortune-tellers. U.S. President Ronald Reagan and his wife, Nancy, believed in astrology. Astrologers watch the stars to predict the future. The Reagans hired astrologers to give them advice on many presidential actions. They thought the stars could guide them to a successful presidency.

2

Piltdown Man

The famous Piltdown Man fossil turned out to be an orangutan's skull.

In the early 1900s, Charles Darwin's theory of evolution was very popular. People began looking for fossils that could be missing links between apes and humans.

In 1912, three men claimed they found one of these missing links near Piltdown, England. The skull looked like an ape's. But it also had human features. The fossil soon became famous around the world.

But the skull was a fake. A German scientist closely examined the skull. He thought it was simply an orangutan's skull. He was right. But people didn't believe him for a long time. Finally, chemical tests in the 1940s proved the bones were really from an orangutan.

THE PILTDOWN CHICKEN

If Piltdown Man wasn't real, how about the Piltdown Chicken? In 1999, *National Geographic* magazine published a story about an amazing fossil from China. It seemed to have the bones of a dinosaur. But it also had wings, feathers, and a beak. Many scientists thought the fossil showed how birds had evolved from dinosaurs.

But the scientists were wrong. Someone had created the fossil by attaching the tail bones of a small dinosaur to a bird skeleton. Of course, *National Geographic* was very embarrassed by its huge mistake!

3

The Cottingley Fairies

Several people believed the Cottingley fairies were real for many years.

In 1917, Elsie Wright and Frances Griffith took some incredible photographs at Cottingley, England. In the photos, the two young girls were smiling and posing with tiny, winged fairies. Their parents showed the photos to a local photography expert. He believed the fairies were the real thing.

Soon all of England went crazy for fairies. The country was recovering from World War I (1914–1918). It had been a nasty and brutal war. The fairy photos gave people hope that there was still good in the world.

HORRIBLE FACT

To create the photos, the girls first cut out several pictures of fairies from a children's book. They used hat pins to hold the pictures up. One girl then posed with the fairies while the other took the picture. The girls created five fake fairy photos this way.

The girls had the support of some famous people. Sir Arthur Conan Doyle, the creator of Sherlock Holmes, believed the fairies were real. Even famous magician Harry Houdini believed the girls. Houdini was a **skeptic** who had exposed many hoaxers of the time. Soon Elsie and Frances, and their fairies, became famous around the world.

For many years, Elsie and Frances defended their claim that the fairies were real. In 1982, they finally admitted that they had faked most of the pictures. But to her dying day, Frances swore that one of the pictures showed real fairies.

skeptic — a person who questions things other people believe

HORRIBLE FACT
The Cottingley fairies have inspired many books, TV shows, and movies.

APRIL FOOL'S!

On April 1, 2007, Dan Baines posted an amazing picture on his Web site in England. The picture showed a dead, shriveled creature. It was about 8 inches (20 centimeters) long. It had gray skin and dried wings. The Web site said the creature was a mummified fairy. Baines assumed people would know it was an April Fool's joke.

But the joke backfired on him. Many people around the world believe fairies are real. Baines was flooded with e-mail messages and phone calls saying he should never move a dead fairy. People scolded him for revealing the fairy's location. Even when he admitted the fake fairy was a prank, people didn't believe him. Instead, they thought the British government was forcing him to keep quiet!

The Great Monkey Hoax

This monkey was claimed to be an alien in 1953.

On July 8, 1953, three young men flagged down a police car near Austell, Georgia. They were very frightened. They claimed they saw a flying saucer as they were speeding down the road. The men said that three weird aliens were standing in the road. They tried to stop, but they hit and killed one of the creatures. The other two aliens ran to their ship and flew away. The men showed the strange, dead creature to the police. It had gray, hairless skin, big eyes, and long arms and legs. It certainly looked like an alien.

But the creature wasn't an alien at all. The young men had made a bet with their friends. They wanted to see who could be the first to get into the newspapers. So they bought a monkey from a pet store and killed it. They cut off its tail and shaved off its hair. Then they just waited for the police. They did get into the papers. But they also paid a large fine for killing the monkey and for making a false police report!

CLEVER CROP CIRCLES

Crop circles are mysterious shapes that sometimes appear in large fields. Some people think aliens are trying to communicate with us through crop circles. But most people think the circles are just clever hoaxes.

One strange crop circle appeared in South Africa in 1993. This crop circle made a familiar shape. It was the logo for the BMW car company. The circle was the clever idea of BMW's advertising agency. The crop circle gave the car company lots of free publicity!

15

Frozen Walt Disney

Walt Disney created Mickey Mouse, Donald Duck, and many other famous characters.

In 1966, Walt Disney died from cancer. His body was cremated, or burned to ashes. But a few years later, rumors began to spread that Disney had wanted to be frozen when he died. The stories said that he wanted to be thawed when a cure for cancer was found.

The rumors about Disney are wrong, though. When Disney died, freezing dead people and reviving them in the future was just a theory. Plus, his cremation is well documented. Still, the stories about frozen Walt live on!

FROZEN FOR THE FUTURE

In order to preserve living tissue, it must be frozen very quickly. Otherwise, ice crystals will destroy the cells. If the cells are destroyed, the tissue stays dead forever. **Cryogenics** is often used to preserve skin, tissue, and organs.

So far, no human being has been successfully frozen and thawed. But some people choose to have their bodies frozen anyway. They hope that scientists might one day be able to revive them and cure their illnesses.

cryogenics — the process of quickly freezing people's bodies when they die

Sir John Mandeville

Mandeville's book described all kinds of amazing creatures.

In 1322, Sir John Mandeville sailed from England. He claimed to have incredible adventures from North Africa to India. He then wrote a book describing his amazing travels. He claimed to have seen a mountain made of gold. He described a race of people with normal bodies and the heads of dogs. He wrote about dragons, sea serpents, and many other fantastic beasts. The book sold well, and at the time, people believed it was true.

However, none of the book's tales were real. Today, most people believe Mandeville's book was based on the adventures of other explorers. Even Mandeville's name is likely fake. There is no official record of anyone named Sir John Mandeville. Nobody knows who actually wrote the book. Yet it inspired many explorers. Even Christopher Columbus believed the book's stories were true.

HOWARD HUGHES

Fake books can mean big business. In 1972, Clifford Irving wrote a biography of Howard Hughes. Hughes was a famous billionaire who had designed several airplanes. He was also very secretive. Hughes was rarely seen in public. However, Irving claimed that he had interviewed Hughes and written a book about his life.

The hoax worked for a while. Irving's book was popular. But eventually, Hughes gave a real interview. He said Irving was a liar. Irving claimed he wrote the book as a joke. But few people believed him.

The Hitler Diaries

On April 25, 1983, the editors at Stern magazine claimed that the Hitler diaries were real.

What would it be like to read the secret thoughts of Adolf Hitler? What if he kept a diary of his crimes during World War II (1939–1945)? How much would people pay to read it? That's just what Konrad Kujau decided to find out.

In the 1970s, Kujau made a living by selling fake Nazi artifacts from World War II. In 1978, Kujau decided to write and sell a fake Hitler diary. Soon a reporter from the German magazine *Stern* offered to buy more of Hitler's diaries.

But Kujau hadn't written any more yet. He made up a story about secretly smuggling the diaries out of East Germany. He claimed lives were in danger and that the magazine had to wait. This gave Kujau time to work on more fake diaries. As time passed, he kept asking for more time and more money. Eventually, Kujau created a total of 60 fake diaries.

In 1983, the magazine presented the complete diaries to a room full of reporters. The editors of *Stern* thought they'd make a lot of money by selling the story. But instead of praise, the skeptical reporters asked many questions. Few believed the diaries were real. The diaries were sent to an expert on World War II documents. The Hitler diaries were soon revealed to be fakes. The expert said the paper and ink used in the diaries was made after the war. Kujau was charged with **fraud** and went to jail for 4 years.

fraud — the practice of cheating or tricking people

HORRIBLE FACT

The Hitler diaries were a costly mistake for *Stern*. The German magazine lost nearly $15 million dollars on the scam. Several editors were also fired for failing to check if the diaries were real.

FAKING A FAKER

After the Hitler diaries scandal, Kujau was a famous man. He was a good artist. When he got out of jail, he began making fakes of famous paintings. He signed his own name so people would know the paintings were fakes. These Kujau Fakes became expensive collectors' items.

After Kujau died, his niece Petra thought she could make money using her uncle's famous name. She signed Kujau's name on cheap copies of famous paintings. Then she sold them for thousands of dollars. People thought they were buying real Kujau Fakes. But they were really buying fake fakes!

Konrad Kujau painted many copies of several famous paintings.

The Kensington Runestone

Most scientists don't believe that the Kensington Runestone was made by the Vikings.

In 1898, Olof Ohman claimed he had found something amazing on his farm near Kensington, Minnesota. It was a large, heavy stone with strange writing carved into it. Ohman said it was tangled up in the roots of a tree on his land. The writing appeared to be ancient Viking **runes**. Was it possible that the Vikings had traveled as far as Minnesota?

runes — an ancient form of writing

Scientists have studied the Kensington Runestone for more than 100 years. They have closely examined the stone and the runes carved into it. Most experts believe the runes were faked. However, a few people believe the stone is proof that the Vikings visited Minnesota long ago.

HORRIBLE FACT

The writing on the Kensington Runestone mentions the year 1362. If the runestone is real, it is proof that the Vikings came to North America more than 100 years before Christopher Columbus!

MORE PROOF?

Several other runestones have been found across the United States. One stone, called the Heavener Runestone, was found in Oklahoma. The runes on the stone refer to the year 1012. Several other stones with runes have also been found nearby. Some researchers believe this is proof that the Vikings were the first settlers of North America. But many historians think it's unlikely the Vikings traveled as far as Oklahoma. They think the runestones are fakes.

Snowball, the Monster Cat

Making fake photos on computers is a popular hobby for many people.

In 2000, an incredible photograph made its way around the world on the Internet. It showed a man holding a giant, fluffy white cat. The cat's name was Snowball. It appeared to be the size of a big dog. The story said that Snowball's parents had lived near an old nuclear power plant. The radiation from the power plant caused Snowball to grow to a huge size.

But the picture and the story weren't true. Cordell Hauglie had made the picture on his home computer. Snowball was chubby, but he was a normal cat. Hauglie sent the fake photo to a few friends as a joke. He had no idea the picture would spread like wildfire over the Internet!

GORGEOUS GUY

The Internet is a perfect playground for hoaxers. In 2001, a picture appeared on a popular Web site of a man waiting for a train. The picture didn't give his name. It simply called him "Gorgeous Guy." Soon the Web site was filled with other "Gorgeous Guy" sightings. Lots of people wondered who the man was. What did he do? And who posted the first picture?

It turns out that "Gorgeous Guy" was Dan Baca. He was a model, and he had posted the pictures himself. Whether he did it to boost his career or just to get attention, no one knew.

Don't Believe Everything!

"There's a sucker born every minute." Famous showman P. T. Barnum is often thought to have started this saying about gullible people. Barnum was a businessman, an entertainer, and an incredible hoaxer.

One of Barnum's most famous hoaxes was the Feejee Mermaid. It had the head and body of a dead monkey and the tail of a dead fish. In 1842, thousands of people paid to see the fake creature.

People can still see the mermaid today. The Barnum Museum in Bridgeport, Connecticut, displays the ugly creature along with many other strange, creepy attractions.

There are a lot of weird things to see in this world. Some are real. But many are fake. The next time you see something strange, remember — seeing isn't always believing!

Visitors can see many odd exhibits at the Barnum Museum.

Glossary

artifact (AR-tuh-fakt) — an object made and used by people in the past

cryogenics (kry-uh-JEN-iks) — the process of quickly freezing people's bodies when they die to preserve them

evolution (ev-uh-LOO-shuhn) — the gradual change of living things over long periods of time

fraud (FRAWD) — the practice of cheating or tricking people

psychic (SYE-kik) — someone who claims to be able to predict the future

radiation (ray-dee-AY-shuhn) — tiny, harmful particles sent out from a radioactive substance

runes (ROONZ) — an ancient form of writing; runes were often carved into large stones.

skeptic (SKEP-tik) — a person who questions things other people believe

Read More

Farndon, John. *Do Not Open: An Encyclopedia of the World's Best-Kept Secrets.* New York: DK Publishing, 2007.

Herbst, Judith. *Hoaxes.* The Unexplained. Minneapolis: Lerner, 2005.

Pascoe, Elaine. *Fooled You! Fakes and Hoaxes Through the Years.* New York: Henry Holt, 2005.

Internet Sites

FactHound offers a safe, fun way to find educator-approved Internet sites related to this book.

Here's what you do:

1. Visit *www.facthound.com*
2. Choose your grade level.
3. Begin your search.

This book's ID number is 9781429622943.

FactHound will fetch the best sites for you!

Index